Sons and Daughters of God:

The time has come!!!

Mboa Marcel, *PhD*
Ndjere Mandon Elise Ariane

1

International Standard Book Number: 9798530584657
Correct® Publishing
Correct® Foundation, P.O. Box: 11265 Yaounde - Cameroon
©2020 by Correct Foundation

 Improve your world, improve the world.

DEDICATION

To those whose careers and businesses are blocked just because they did not conform to the patterns of this world.

INTRODUCTION

Christian leadership to improve the world.

The fact that the children of God are confined to roles of secondary importance in our society is just like the servitude of a prince in his father's kingdom. A curious paradox of the slave-prince which the Bible clearly explains in the book of Galatians 4:1 *"...The heir, as long as he is a child, differeth nothing from a servant, though he be lord of all"*

Nowadays, in our societies, the paradox of the slave-prince is of salient prevalence, as satan's followers hold prominent positions. We, the worthy sons of God and Father of our Lord Jesus Christ, have chosen to remain servants, whereas we are the master of everything, according to the revealed Word and will of God. We have abandoned power, wealth and glory to the sons of the son of rebellion who constantly try to persuade us to join them on the side of the fallen archangel. This unfortunate situation must come to an end. The time has come!!! The time has come to grow!!! The time has come for the Sons and Daughters of God to become the masters of everything in this world!!!

The state and functioning of the world will experience a bit of improvement only if divinity meets humanity in those holding positions of significant influence. And it is exactly this dual nature of humanity and divinity that we, Sons and Daughters of God, have inherited from our Lord Jesus Christ. We are therefore the ones to improve on the state and functioning of the world. It is our duty to improve all things on earth. Obviously, we can better fulfil this duty by ascending to positions of significant influence ourselves; as those holding such positions now have already, for most of them, sworn allegiance to satan.

The brochure you are reading is the substance of Divine revelation. It is not the result of human thought. God has revealed that He has taken the resolution to raise His chosen ones to positions of significant influence in all institutions determining the state and functioning of the world, States and Churches inclusive. God says *"The time has come"* for His children to ascend to the highest positions in International Organisations, Companies, Administrations, States and their institutions, as well as in Religious Organisations. To get ready, He teaches His chosen ones who will soon be promoted to these high positions. This is done through two (02) messages: the keys to Divine Elevation (Message I) and God's power is enough for our challenges (Message II). These messages are followed by seven confessions inspired by God, in order to strengthen the faith of those elected.

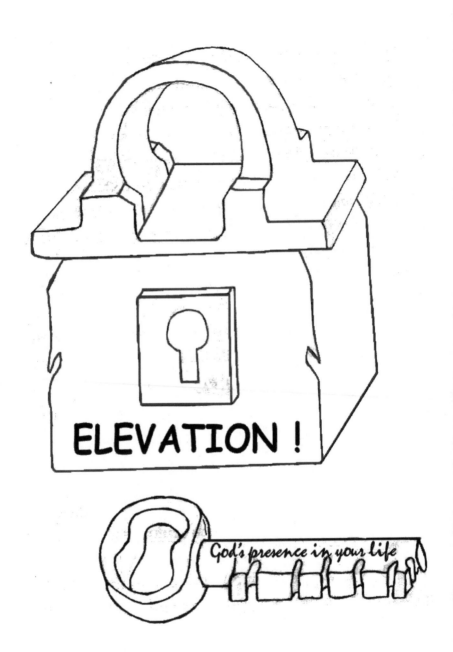

ELEVATION !

God's presence in your life

MESSAGE I

THE KEYS TO DIVINE ELEVATION

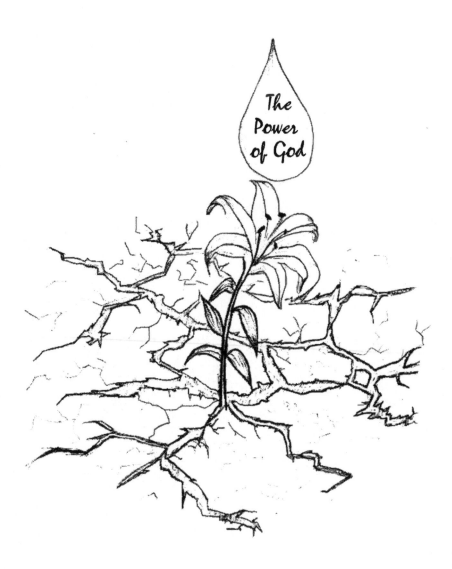

ELEVATION COMES FROM GOD AND IS FOR GOD

The Bible, which is God's Word and Will revealed to mankind, tells us that *"Promotion cometh neither from the east, nor from the west, nor from the south. But God is the judge: he putteh down one, and setteh up another" (Psalms 75:6-7), and that "The most High ruleth in the kingdom of men, and giveth it to whomsoever he will."* (Daniel 4:25)

We also know that the enemy, the devil/satan, recruits his followers through seduction, just as we know that he excels in imitation, a kind of fake which is very close to the original. In this regard, let us remember that he succeeded in replicating three of the ten signs and miracles God performed in Egypt in order to convince Pharaoh to free His people (Exodus, chapters 7 to 12). Subsequently, it becomes necessary to be able to recognise promotion that originates from God. The Sons and Daughters of God, that is, those who are born again, must know that promotion comes from God and is for God (1), that God systematically gives instructions to those He promotes (2), and that distinction should be made between promotion coming from God and the one surreptitiously offered by the imitator and master seducer, the devil (3).

Promotion comes from God

God starts promoting us to show that He has swung into action. That is what He did with Joshua, His servant. The Bible teaches us that the Lord said to Joshua: *"This day will I begin to magnify thee in the sight of all Israel, that they may know that, as I was with Moses, so I will be with thee"* (Joshua 3:7). For God, the true promoter, to be recognised unequivocally and His glory not attributed to whomsoever, God promotes distinctively. He makes His sons and daughters get unexpected positions, which they would never have dreamt of and which they would never have got except thanks to Him, God.

⌛ He took Joseph, a Jewish slave sold by his own brothers (Genesis 37:28) and a prisoner (Genesis

39:20), and promoted him to the position of Vice King of Egypt (Genesis 41: 43).

⧗ He took Moses, a child abandoned in the reeds by the side of a river (Exodus 2: 3), and promoted to the position of leader/liberator of the people of Israel in captivity in Egypt.

⧗ He took Daniel, a captive of Judah on exile (Daniel 1: 3) and made of him the third personality of the Government of the Kingdom of Babylon (Daniel 5:29).

⧗ He took David, a shepherd (1 Samuel 16:11-13) and positioned him as the king of the house of Judah (2 Samuel 2:4).

The people of Israel are reminded of God's intervention in the following terms: *"For the LORD your God dried up the waters of the Jordan from before you, until ye were passed over, as the LORD your God did to the Red sea, which he dried up from before us, until we were* gone over: *That all the people of the earth might know the hand of the LORD, that it is mighty: that ye might fear the LORD your God for ever"* (Joshua 4:23-24).

It is therefore important to avoid relying on men or attributing our promotion to anybody else because that dilutes the Glory of God. We, Sons and Daughters of God, should *"cease ye from man, whose breath is in his nostrils: for wherein is he to be accounted of?"* (Isaiah 2:22). God repeatedly prevents us from comparing His works to those of a man and makes us know that He does not share His Glory in the book of Isaiah 46 verse 5: *"To whom will ye liken me, and make me equal, and compare me, that we may like?"*

Promotion is for God

God promotes us first for Himself and, incidentally, for ourselves. That is what He reminds us of in the book of Isaiah when He says, *"For mine own sake, even for mine own sake, will I do it: for how should my name be polluted? And I will not give my glory unto another"* (Isaiah 48:11). For God to elevate us for Himself, it is necessary for our relationship with Him to be known publicly. It must be clearly established that we are of God, the true God and Father of our Lord Jesus Christ. We must affirm our Christianity without any restriction or reservation. That way, as He cannot let His followers lag behind or be oppressed, He gets into action to elevate them, not for them (His followers), but for Himself because anything associated with the name of God must be for His glory and His magnificence. It therefore becomes counter-productive to try to hide one's Christianity or mention any lack of merit, following a promotion we believe comes from God.

God's promotion comes with the necessary skills

When God promotes us, He gives us the necessary skills. He gave them to Moses when He sent him to go and save His people from Pharaoh's oppression. Eventhough moses tried to mention his disability; namely his language difficulties, to dodge the mission God was entrusting him with, the LORD said unto him,

"Who hath made man's mouth? Or who maketh the dumb, or deaf, or the seeing, or the blind? Have not I the LORD? Now therefore go, and I will be with thy mouth, and teach thee what thou shalt say" (Exodus 4:11-12). It is therefore useless trying to look for supernatural powers elsewhere because God endows us with His power to achieve our mission in the new position we have been promoted to.

Knowing that promotion comes from God, the son of God, who benefits from it, must listen very attentively to Him in order to receive instructions related to his promotion. This is for God to be magnified to the fullest through the distinctive tenure of the granted position.

ELEVATION FROM GOD COMES WITH INSTRUCTIONS

The Bible teaches us that everything man/woman does glorifies either the true God, Father of our Lord Jesus Christ, or the devil/satan (the enemy). Good actions glorify God, and bad actions glorify the enemy. Having been elevated by God and for the glory of God, the child of God must devote himself to glorifying God in this grace and in his life (1) ; he must avoid compromising himself (2) and must make sure he is not spiritually weak (3). Such are the instructions God attaches to his elevation.

Glorifying God in this grace and in one's life

The first instruction which God gives His children He elevates is to glorify Him through their actions and behaviour, not only as they carry out their new duties but in their lives in general. The children of God must make sure their new position does not bring about their fall. They must lead a life which glorifies God. By doing this, they avoid all sorts of trials and tribulations and get their civil, penal or moral responsibility less involved. By leading an honest life which glorifies God, they avoid any kind of fall. Elevation implies, majesty, glory and honour (Daniel 5:18-19), but it can also quickly lead to ruin when we lose sight of the requirement to act for the glory of God and the happiness of men. That is what happened to king Nebuchadnezzar and to his successor, Belshazzar (Daniel 5:18-31). A child of God must avoid that his promotion lifts his heart up and/or hardens his spirit in pride, in order not to be deposed from his throne, and his glory taken away from him (Daniel 5:20). Having this in mind and acting accordingly the son or daughter of God moves from promotion to promotion, and never from ascent to descent; God being more and more glorified.

Not compromising oneself

The second instruction God gives His chosen ones is to remain faithful to Him, at this time when all kinds of dishonourable behaviour are significantly threatening this faithfulness. God's demand is that elevation should not make His children lose spiritual integrity. It is all about avoiding worshipping fake gods, mainly represented in our era by all sorts of satanic sects. We earlier saw that the devil/satan, recruits through seduction. Now, if it is relatively easier to refuse to join these works of darkness (satanic sects and magical practices) when the offer to join is in exchange for a brighter future, it is less easier to resist when we are faced with the threat of losing a position we have already been promoted to. The child of God must remain firm. This firmness shall be based on the conviction that his elevation comes from God and Father of our Lord Jesus Christ, and not from a man or any great master. The elevated child of God shall emulate Daniel who rejected the king's enticing promises because accepting them could distort God's glory when he would be promoted in the future: *"Then Daniel answered and said before the king, Let thy gifts be to thyself, and give thy rewards to another"* (Daniel 5:17). Thus, when the child of God shall be faced with the threat of making him lose his position or duties if he does not join such and such satanic sect, he shall have to be as courageous as Daniel to say, *"Let thy gifts be to thyself, and give thy rewards to another"*, knowing he shall obtain the same result Daniel obtained: *"Then commanded Belshazzar, and they clothed Daniel with scarlet, and put a chain of gold about his neck, and made a proclamation concerning him, that he should be the third ruler in the kingdom"* (Daniel 5:29). Any faithfulness to God is highly rewarded by God Who, Himself, is perfectly faithful.

Not being spiritually weak

There is an unchanging law stipulating that in man/woman, there is a negative correlation between the flesh (the natural man's will and thoughts geared towards doing evil) and the spirit (man's divine nature geared towards doing good). The heavier the flesh, the weaker the spirit. The Bible explains that *"For the flesh lusteth against the Spirit, and the Spirit against the flesh: and these are contrary the one to the other: so that ye cannot do the things that ye would"* (Galatians 5:17). Being spiritually weak simply means remaining attached to the desires of the flesh and refusing to renew one's mind in order to uplift oneself spiritually. Now, spiritual elevation is the precondition for any other form of elevation. Without spiritual elevation, the child of God will have a lot of difficulties to cope with his elevation in the world. The last instruction which God attaches to his elevation is to kill the flesh so as to give room for the spirit by living according to His Word because (1) *"It is the Spirit that quickeneth"*, (2) *"the flesh profiteth nothing"* and (3) *"the words that I speak unto you, they are spirit, and they are life"* (John 6:63). An example of somebody whom elevation rendered weak spiritually and made the flesh heavy is King Belshazzar. Interpreting a vision of this king, Daniel told him *"Thou hasth lifted up thyself against the Lord of heaven; and they have brought the vessels of his house before thee, and thou, and thy lords, thy wives, and thy concubines, have drunk wine in them; and thou hast praised the gods of silver, and gold, of brass, iron, wood and stone, which see not, nor hear, nor know: and the God in whose hand thy breath is, and whose are all thy ways, hast thou not glorified"* (Daniel 5:23). Those elevated by God must therefore avoid being spiritually weak, and using their elevation as Belshazzar did.

Before attributing one's elevation to God and receiving related instructions, it is advisable to know how to distinguish the promotion which comes from the true God and which leads to wealth, glory and life from the one which comes from the master seducer, the devil/satan, and leads to wealth, glory and... death.

HOW TO RECOGNISE ELEVATION WHICH COMES FROM GOD

The Bible teaches us that *"The blessing of the Lord, it maketh rich, and he addedth no sorrow with it"* (Proverbs 10:22). The first sign of elevation from God is the absence of sacrifice in exchange for promotion. Grievous sacrifices before or after a promotion clearly show that it comes from the devil/satan, lord of the followers of satanic sects who worship the devil, sometimes using Jesus' name. In addition to this sign, promotion from God is generally an event of outstanding importance: (1) God blesses you regardless of the context and circumstances, and (2) God elevates you amidst your enemies and allows you to reign over them.

God blesses you regardless of the context and circumstances

When God enters into action, the context and circumstances lose their prominence. It is important to know it, first to build our belief when we hope for a promotion from God, then to convince ourselves that the said promotion comes from God. Whether the child of God is ostracised by the numerous satanic brotherhoods in our organisations and institutions or he is automatically excluded by the context and circumstances does not matter much: the hand of God is stronger to elevate those who belong to Him. Daniel's example is instructive about this. While interpreting King Belshazzar's vision, he could accept the king's donations or presents and give his vision an interpretation which would please the king. He could, by fear for retaliation, pretend to give an interpretation which would spare him from the king's anger. But despite the context and circumstances which imposed complaisance on him, he gave the interpretation which he had received from God; with the certainty he would not get anything from what the king had promised him. It was without considering that God would go into action: surprisingly, he was clothed with scarlet (wealth and high dignity), given the golden necklace (purity and majesty), given the third position in the government of the kingdom, not to mention that his life was safe (Daniel 5:29). Any elevation which comes from God defies logical, contextual and circumstantial reasoning, and pertains to the realm of wonders. It surprises everybody, including enemies, adversaries, spoilsport and the like.

 God elevates us amidst our enemies and allows us to reign over them

The Bible teaches us that *"When a man's ways pleases the LORD, he maketh even his enemies to be at peace with him"* (Proverbs 16:7). When God decides to elevate you, He imposes His resolution to decision makers in the physical world. It does not matter whether these authorities abhor us. God will make us find favour with them as He did for Joseph (Act 7:10), and they will sign the decree/decision, surprised by the fear and the fright of the powerful hand of God (Exodus 15:16). Let us come back to Daniel's example to observe that he was made the third highest personality in the kingdom of Babylon, amidst and to the detriment of magicians, astrologers, Chaldeans and soothsayers who were his opponents in that situation, because they were working for other gods than the true God (Daniel 5:11). The child of God is promoted by his Heavenly Father among the followers of the most popular satanic sects because God controls the rule of men.

In this revealed message, we have expounded that God promotes for a longer time than the enemy (the devil/satan) does, contrary to what our rulers/leaders want to make us believe. It is not necessary to join sects and devilish brotherhoods to be promoted to high positions in our organisations and institutions. To calm down His wrath this 2020, God is looking for faithful men and women to place at the head of institutions which determine the state and functioning of the world. Faithful children of God must prepare to be promoted to high places in our administrations, companies and other national and international organisations. For this reason, we, followers of God, must:

⧗ learn to recognise elevation that comes from God, in order to be able to reject seductive promotions coming from the devil;

⌛ Understand that no elevation matters if it is not from God and for God because God gives the related skills and blesses the fruits;

⌛ Devote ourselves to making promotion an opportunity to serve God and the Glory of God.

God wants His children to be promoted to positions of power and to reign over the followers of satan who have led the world to its deplorable state we see it today. For this purpose, He makes His power available and sufficient to face the challenges related to these new positions, to this new ministry. It is left to each of us to enter into a new commitment with God.

MESSAGE II

THE POWER OF GOD IS SUFFICIENT FOR OUR CHALLENGES

 GOD PREPARES HIS CHILDREN FOR PROMOTION

When God decides to elevate His child, He prepares him and equips him well. He refuels him, like a ship or plane, in order to maintain life on board, planning for meteorological hazards. The child of God has what it takes to sail through when faced with some turbulence and unfavourable tides. It is needless looking for other sources of power in order to be successful in the new position. God recalls that through the mouth of prophet Isaiah talking to Hezekiah, King of Judah totally panicking in front of the super powerful army of Sancherib, King of Assyria, who was planning to eat Judas and Jerusalem for breakfast in less than no time: *"Hast thou not heard long ago, how I have done it; and of ancient times, that I have formed it? Now have I brought it to pass, that thou shouldest be to lay waste defenced cities into ruinous heaps"* (Isaiah 37:26). The child of God must not get worked up or be afraid of the punishment or shame promised by members of the most violent and discriminatory sect brotherhoods. The only thing to do is to be firm, refusing to compromise oneself, and to turn to God. It seems there are administrations/ organisations out there where one can hear that *"there is no God here!!!"*, thus referring everybody to great masters of satanic sects, to people practising all sorts of magic (black, white, grey, etc.), and to soothsayers and other great masters of traditional rites which God prevents his children from doing in Deuteronomy 18:9-11 when he says: ***"... thou shalt not learn to do after the abominations of those nations. There shall not be found among you any one that maketh his son or his daughter pass through the fire, or that useth divination, or an observer of times, or an enchanter, or a witch, Or a charmer, or a consulter with familiar spirits, or a wizard, or a necromancer".*** This ***"There is no God here!!!"*** resembles the message which the king of Assyria sent to Hezekiah, King of Judah, to convince him to surrender, given the imbalance of the armed forces which was unfavourable to the latter: ***"...let not thy God, in whom thou trustest, deceive thee,*** *saying, Jerusalem shall not be given into the hand of the king of Assyria"* (Isaiah 37:10). We know what happened next. The Bible tells us that *"Then the angel of the LORD went forth, and smote in the camp of the Assyrians a hundred and fourscore and five thousand: and when they arose early in the morning, behold, they were all dead corpses",* and Sennacherib, King of Assyria, lost the war and the throne (Isaiah 37:36-37).

The child of God is prepared for his new position, and all the challenges he has to face are not meant for his failure or downfall but for the glory of God because the child of God does not fight for victory; he fights in victory.

K THE CHILD OF GOD DOES NOT FIGHT FOR VICTORY, HE FIGHTS IN VICTORY

Carrying out one's duties amidst a perverted and corrupt generation adds to adversity. Adversity is spiritual, not physical *"For we wrestle not against flesh and blood, but against principalities, against powers, against the rulers of darkness of this world, against spiritual wickedness in high places"* (Ephesians 6:12). That is why we do not fight standing and shouting but rather on our knees in the silence of prayer. Silence is the rule here because it means serenity and assurance of victory. It is all about being quiet and focused on prayer. That is what Moses called on the people of Israel to do when he told them: *"...fear ye not, stand still, and see the salvation of the LORD, which he will shew to you today: for the Egyptians whom ye have seen today, ye shall see them again no more for ever. The LORD shall fight for you, and ye shall hold your peace"* (Exodus 14:13-14). It is also silence that King Hezekiah recommended to his representatives when faced with the pressing threats of the king of Assyria: *"...answer him not"* (Isaiah 36:21). The instruction God gives His chosen ones is not to panic when faced with adversity, but to be quiet because their victory is guaranteed; because Jesus Christ, *"...having spoiled principalities and powers, he made a shew of them openly, triumphing over them in it"* (Colossians 2:15). Silence is the rule and *"if a man also strive for masteries, yet is he not crowned, except he strive lawfully"* (2 Timothy 2:5).

When carrying out our new duties, many will come to us to try to discredit God in our eyes and show us the limits of His power in this world controlled by the devil/satan, as the king of Assyria did to the people of Judah (Isaiah 10, 15, and 20). We shall simply not answer them. We shall withdraw, pray and, if need be, call for a man of God (preferably a prophet), as Hezekiah did when threatened by the king of Assyria (Isaiah 37:14-22, 36). The result will be the same. We shall be victorious, just as King Hezekiah did.

At the end of this second revealed message, it

appears that God prepares His children appropriately for their new duties, which they shall carry out for His greatest glory. We do not need to join sects, devilish brotherhoods or secret societies in which traditional rites are done, in order to have the necessary power to carry out our duties well in these perverted and corrupt places which our administrations, our companies and other National and International Organisations of all kinds happen to be. The power of God is sufficient. For this reason, the followers of God that we are must:

⌛ Understand and admit that we are prepared and equipped enough to successfully carry out our present and future duties;

⌛ Know and believe that we are automatically victorious in the battles our new positions prepare us for and that we do not need to use non-conventional means to fight.

God has arranged everything for our elevation to be for His greatest glory, for our own happiness and the happiness of a greater number of people in our area of influence. His power and His guidance are available for us. Let us lean only on them. To build our faith, let us confess and believe the revealed messages he gives us below.

STANDING ON GOD'S PROMISES

38

CONCLUSION

 (RECOMMENDED CONFESSIONS)

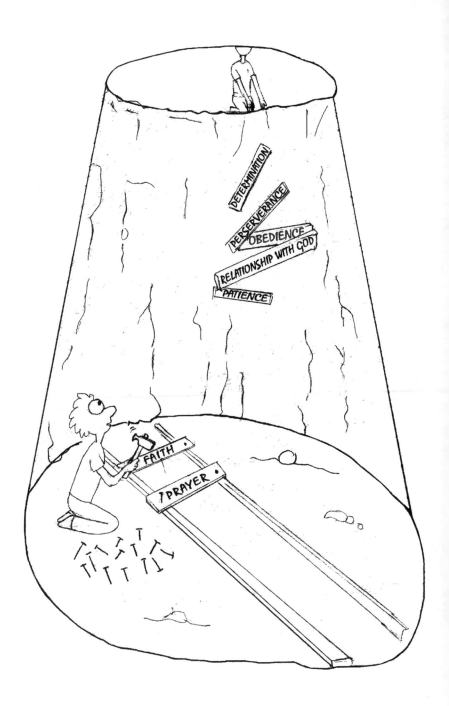

RECOMMENDED CONFESSIONS

1. God frees me in Jesus-Christ and takes all spiritual weight off me and all mental burden which prevent me from rising up to His intentions for me, in Jesus-Christ's name!!!

2. God works in me both to will and to do of His good pleasure in order to keep a deep relationship with Him, in Jesus-Christ's name!!!

3. God uses me and makes my life a tool for His splendour and His glory, in Jesus-Christ's name!!!

4. God fortifies me and renews my strength in the face of adversity. He guarantees my victory through an excellent spiritual preparation based on tests and trials, in Jesus-Christ's name!!!

5. God makes me find favour in Him and any other person. And my favour is beneficial to a greater

number of people in my growing area of influence, in Jesus-Christ's name!!!

6. God breaks the sticks of wicked people and the rod of rulers against me. I am not afraid of them and I am not afraid of their speeches. They shall know no peace against me, in Jesus-Christ's name!!!

7. God sets me free from those who wage a war against me because I refuse to join devilish sects and orders. They shall not see me fall, in Jesus-Christ's name!!!

Glory for ever be to God the Father of any favour in Jesus Christ's name. Amen!!!

WHERE DOES
SUCCESS COME FROM ?

CORRECT FOUNDATION *Improve your world, improve the world.*

Made in the USA
Middletown, DE
11 March 2022